FOOD

ANNE SCHRAFF

P.O. Box 355, Buena Park, CA 90621

www.artesianpress.com

Nonfiction
eXtreme Customs Series

Editor: John Bonaccorsi
Project Coordinator: Cynthia Sevilla
Graphic Design: Tony Amaro
Cover Photo: Fujiko
©2006 Artesian Press

www.artesianpress.com

 Artesian **Press**   ISBN 1-58659-214-9

Contents

Word List

Arawak (AR-eh-wak) Native people of Guyana, on the coast of South America.

baklava (bah-kleh-VAH) A dessert made of thin pastry, nuts, and honey.

bierkase (beer-kase-a) A strong-smelling German cheese made from beer.

Cayenne (ky-EN) A strong, orange-red to dark-red ground pepper.

couscous (KOOS-koos) A dish that is made from a hard wheat flour called semolina and is usually served along with meat or vegetables.

delicatessen (deh-lih-keh-TEH-sehn) A shop selling and/or serving ready-to-eat food products, such as meats, cheeses, and salads.

diniguan (din-ih-GWAN) A Philippine stew made of pig blood and pig meat or parts.

durian (DER-ee-an) A large, oval, tasty but foul-smelling fruit with a prickly rind.

escargot (es-KAR-go) A snail prepared for use as food.

fugu (FOO-goo) A poisonous puffer fish used as a food in Japan after the toxic organs are removed.

garum (GAH-rum) A Roman sauce made from salted fish.

geophagy (JEE-uh-feh-jee) Eating earthy substances, such as clay, because the normal diet is poor or doesn't have enough vitamins and minerals.

gusano (goo-SA-no) A kind of worm that is put in tequila drinks.

habanero (hah-beh-NARE-oh) A small, bright-green pepper that is very hot.

haggis (HA-gehs) A Scottish dish in which the heart, liver, and lungs of a sheep or calf are chopped up with onions, fat, oatmeal, and seasonings and then boiled in the stomach of the animal.

hakarl (how-carrhl) Fermented shark meat eaten in Iceland.

haute cuisine (oat kwee- ZEEN) A French term for frying food or cooking. It means "high cooking."

Herodotus (He-ROD-oh-tus) an ancient Greek historian.

irn bru (ern broo) A bright orange Scottish drink that tastes like bubblegum and is served with haggis.

jalapeño (hal-leh-PAY-nyo) A small, fat dark green Mexican hot pepper.

kare-kare (KAR-ay KAR-ay) A meaty oxtail stew with vegetables and pieces of tender tripe in peanut sauce. A Pillipino dish.

kielbasa (kill-BAH-suh) A spicy smoked polish sausage.

luau (LOO-ow) A Hawaiian feast.

Papua New Guinea (PA-pyew-eh noo GIN-ee) A country in the western Pacific Ocean, north of Australia.

pemmican (PEH-mih-kehn) Lean, dried meat, pounded and mixed with melted fat. It was a food of North American Indians.

pierogies (per-O-gees) Dough filled with potatoes, cheese, or other items. A Polish food.

pilli-pilli (PIL-ee PIL-ee) A kind of African seasoning that is stronger than cayenne pepper.

pizzerias (PEET-seh-ree-ehz) Places where pizzas are made and sold.

6

Poi (poy) A paste made from taro root. A Hawiian food.

rennin (REH-nehn) An enzyme used in making cheese from milk.

sappari (sa-PA-ree) A Japanese word meaning clean, light, and refreshing.

sashimi (sa-SHEE-mee) A Japanese dish of thinly-sliced raw fish.

scrapple Meat scraps cooked in corn meal and fried, often served with eggs.

seviche (seh-VEE-chay) A Mexican raw fish marinated in lime or lemon juice, with oil, onions, peppers, and various seasonings.

shish-kebab (SHISH-keh-bob) Alternating pieces of meat and vegetables broiled on skewers.

sushi (SOO-shee) Small cakes of cooked, cold rice topped with slices of raw fish.

tallow (TA-loe) The white, nearly-tasteless solid fat of cattle, sheep, and deer.

tortilla (tor-TEE-uh) A thin, round pancake made from cornmeal or flour and then cooked on a griddle.

wasabi (wah-SAH-bee) A condiment made from an Asian root that is like horseradish.

Chapter 1

Everybody Needs Food

During the Great Depression of the 1930s, when life was very hard for people, a hungry young mother in the Midwest looked up into a tree and wished she could eat the leaves. She looked down at all the weeds, which were growing everywhere. One weed, the dandelion, which means "lion's tooth," looked as if might taste good. The woman was so hungry, she snatched up the weed's green leaves, added some vinegar, and for the next few months lived on dandelions and a few potatoes. It turned out dandelions are very nutritious.

As a history of food shows, weeds are not the strangest things people have eaten. Sometimes they eat things that are not meant for food at all. When they eat earthy things, for instance, it is called geophagy (JEE-uh-feh-jee), and it has happened for thousands of years.

Strange things—strange to us—are eaten all over the world. Having blood pudding and jellied eels washed down with warm beer for dinner might not sound delicious to Americans, but it used to be a popular dish in England. In Scotland, a sheep's stomach is stuffed with chopped-up heart, liver, and lungs and then steamed. This dish is called haggis (HA-gehs), and it is served with irn bru (ern broo), a bright orange drink that tastes like bubblegum. Norway is known for lutefisk, dried codfish that is soaked in lye before it is cooked. In the Netherlands, people think salted horsemeat sandwiches go well with raw salted fish, called herring. The Dutch put peanut-butter sauce on their french fries.

In Mediterranean countries, an entire sheep's head, including the eyeballs, might be served, along with octopus and squid in their own ink. Blood is drunk fresh from the neck veins of live cattle in some parts

At a market in Turkey, sheep heads are for sale.

©Hiro Miyazawa

of Africa. This does not seriously harm the animal. Rancid, or slightly spoiled, yak milk is popular in Tibet, which is part of Asia. Sage worms are eaten in the island country of Papua New Guinea (PA-pyew-eh noo GIN-ee), in the western Pacific Ocean.

China has a wide variety of unusual dishes, including the amazing bird's-nest soup. A small bird called a swallow gathers twigs and grass and builds its nest, gluing it together with a jelly-like substance that the bird spits up. After the young birds have flown away, people gather the empty nests and clean them. After the nests are rinsed, all that is left is the gooey jelly. The jelly is then simmered, and bird's-nest soup is the result. It has a delicate fish flavor and is a

These garden snails might be someone's meal.

very popular delicacy.

The Chinese also enjoy jelled blood. It is made from duck or pig blood formed into a salty mold that looks like a jelly dessert. In southeast Asia, durian (DER-ee-an), a football-sized fruit, is eaten. The tough outer skin covers pale yellow flesh. Though the taste of durian is considered marvelous, the odor of the fruit has been compared with that of a dead animal rotting in the sun.

Fried escargot (es-KAR-go) are broiled garden snails and are a treat in many parts of the world. Germany is famous for having incredibly stinky cheeses. Limburger cheese smells so strong it can make an entire house stink. Yet another German cheese, bierkase

12

(beer-kase-a), is made from beer and also has a powerful smell.

John the Baptist, of Bible days, is said to have lived on locusts and wild honey. The Roman naturalist Pliny noted that the locust was much enjoyed in Rome. Greek historian Herodotus (He-ROD-oh-tus) described how locusts were baked into cakes, adding to their taste and texture. Unknown to them, most people eat many insects during their lifetime. Beetles and weevils end up in our bread. The tiny black specks we might see in flour are probably parts of their bodies. Small grubs hide in fruits and vegetables. Many apple growers turn bug-infested fruit into cider.

The insects that get into our diet do no harm. In fact, they are a healthy, low-fat source of protein. There are 12.9 grams of protein in a hundred grams of crickets, which also have calcium, phosphorus (FOS-fer-es), iron, thiamin, riboflavin, niacin, and only 5.5 grams of fat. The same amount of beef has the same nutrients but over 21 grams of fat.

A bowl of crickets is healthier than a steak. The insects eaten in an African desert, the burnt sea slugs eaten in Vietnam, and the lemon ants served in Ecuador are not such a bad idea.

Chapter 2

Food of Ancient Peoples

Artist's Depiction: Fujiko

The Mammoth was related to the elephant. It was once hunted by man.

When human beings lived in caves, they did not have the opportunity to choose foods that looked delicious. They had to eat whatever they could find, or they would starve.

In the beginning, humans ate everything raw. Early men hunted reindeer, bison, rhinoceros, and woolly mammoths. The women gathered seeds and berries and dug

15

for roots. The people were nomadic, which means they moved around a lot, following herds of migrating animals. They were like the animals, in that they spent most of their waking hours looking for something to eat.

The idea of roasting meat probably arose by accident. We can imagine or guess that a caveman accidentally dropped some meat into the fire. When he pulled it out, he most likely burned his fingers. He probably put his greasy fingers into his mouth and sucked on them to ease the pain. It could have been his first contact with the delicious flavor of juicy, roasted meat.

Early people believed food had magical powers. When they ate parts of an animal, they thought the different organs would give them new skills and powers. Eating a bull's tail was believed to give courage since bulls were brave, while eating the brains of clever animals made a man wise. By eating an animal's liver, a man gained strength-or so he believed.

Many cave dwellers chose to live near

lakes and rivers so they could find fish to eat. As people gathered near water, they found they could plant seeds that would grow into things they could eat. For the first time, a hungry man could look to his garden for food and did not have to eat only grubs or worms when the meat was gone.

People planted wheat and barley and slowly turned wild sheep, cattle, goats, and pigs into farm animals. Diets improved as the food source became more dependable. People learned to grind grain into flour, but they did not yet know how to make bread. The flour became porridge, which is like thick, hot cereal; other times, it was made into unleavened scones, a kind of flat biscuit. For the first time in history, humans had something to eat that was different from wild berries, seeds, insects, and the flesh of animals. If a family were hungry, it could kill one of it's own animals or pick food from the garden. The cows gave milk, another valuable food.

Milk has been used as food throughout

history, and it does not come from cows only. Sheep and goats, as well as cows, provide milk through Europe and North America. Reindeer are the source of milk in Lapland. The water buffalo provides milk in India and other parts of Asia, as does the llama in the Andes Mountains of South America.

Cheese was also discovered in ancient times. A legend tells the tale of an Arabian or Persian horseman who filled his saddlebag with milk and flung it over his horse. The pouch was made from leather and the lining of a calf's stomach. After a long, hot ride, the man tried to drink some of the milk. A watery liquid came out. Inside the pouch, he found a strange white lump. A chemical called rennin (REH-nehn) had acted on the milk and curdled it into cheese. A new food was born.

About 6,000 years ago in southeast Asia, a wide variety of foods became part of the human diet. People were eating almonds, beans, betel nuts, cucumbers, peas, as well as melons. They learned to grow rice, to salt

Wealthy ancient Greeks lying back and eating

meat, and to store both for the times when not much food could grow.

The Greeks invented the sack lunch. When they went to the theater, they brought along bread, olives, and cheese to eat with their wine during the long performances. Wealthy Greeks often lay back on couches to eat, using their fingers to pick up their food. Bread was always served, and it was used like a napkin to wipe one's mouth and fingers. The poor in Greece hardly ever ate meat or fish. They lived on stews made from peas and beans. They also made a flatbread called maza from grain paste. If they were lucky, they were able to make it taste better by adding cheese, olives, eggs, figs, or grapes.

Greek soldiers and sailors ate tasteless barley-paste cakes and water. Few persons in Greece ate more than one main meal, which was eaten at night. For breakfast and lunch, they just snacked.

The Spartans of Greece were famous for their bravery and being willing to die on the battlefield, but they were not known for tasty food. They made a black broth from pork stock, salt, and vinegar. One visitor who tried this Spartan soup said that it was so awful he could understand why the Spartans went so willingly to battle. This visitor swore he would rather jump in the river than drink another drop of the broth.

The Romans also relaxed on couches or pillows when they ate. Their cooks were usually men. One emperor got the entire Roman senate together to tell his cooks how to prepare a large fish. Another had dinner menus sewn in fancy letters on the tablecloths used for his banquets. One time, he and his

Artist's Depiction: Fujiko

A dormouse was a popular snack in ancient Rome.

guests ate the brains of six hundred ostriches at a single meal. Guests who overate at great meals solved the problem by simply throwing up to empty their stomachs. After doing that, they could begin eating all over again.

Great dinners were held in rooms with temporary ceilings. At a certain signal, the ceilings would open, and the guests would be showered with tons of rose petals. Once, four guests suffocated when too many rose petals buried them.

A popular menu item throughout Rome was an animal called a dormouse, cooked in honey and poppy seeds. A very powerful sauce called garum (GAH-rum) was made with salted fish. It could cover up the bad taste of just about anything. If they could afford it, Romans enjoyed baked eggs and cheese, as well as boiled bacon with cabbage and mint. Hanging from hooks in well-stocked Roman kitchens were the salted and pickled bodies of rabbits and wild birds, waiting to become part of a meal. Poor Romans had to be satisfied with gruel, which was a thin porridge, and whatever meat scraps they could beg.

Flattened mice were a special favorite, along with small birds, such as thrushes. In their gardens, most Romans kept milk-fed snails to be eaten. The snails became so fat that they almost burst from their shells. A kind of ice cream was made by mixing snow with flour and sweet white wine. Peacock brains and ostrich and flamingo tongues were eaten, too. Tiny cooked birds were stuffed with many spices before being eaten. The Romans also hunted deer and wild boar.

Roman cooks liked to mix sweet and salty

foods. The most popular meat was salted pork.

Food preparation and arranging were an art in Rome, as they are in many parts of the world today. The Romans did not want their food to be tasty only; they wanted it to look good. It had to be presented attractively and artistically.

The Romans were not the only ancient people who had huge feasts. In Persia, a king once had one thousand animals killed for a single banquet. In China, a rich man served forty different dishes at one meal. Examples included such tasty treats as well-roasted grasshoppers, snakes, elephant feet, bear paws, and the lips and brains of monkeys. Cooks were widely honored throughout the ancient world, and a cook who was able to present an exotic and memorable feast could become a rich man.

Chapter 3

Medieval Munchies

The Vikings, who lived in what is now the Scandinavian peninsula, mixed barley and oats to make the porridge that was a main part of their diet. They would also eat huge quantities of salted sheep and pigs. They made it taste better by adding garlic, mustard, and honey.

When the medieval period began around 500 AD, there was a big difference in the way the poor and the rich ate. Sailors, usually poor boys who went to sea because they had no choice, lived on something called ship's biscuits. These were made from a flour and water mix that was baked and dried until it was rock hard. These biscuits could be kept for 50 years and still be eaten. During long sea voyages, the sailors soaked the biscuits in water until they broke up into a kind of mushy cereal. This was eaten with salted pork or fish in vinegar. Sailors might have sometimes waited until dark to eat, so that they would not see the maggots crawling around in their food. Cheese eaten around this time was often full of hair, insects, and other disgusting things.

For most persons in the medieval period, breakfast was rye bread and cheese. Lunch was the same. For the main meal in the late afternoon or evening, the poor ate a thick onion soup, baked beans, or peas porridge, which was a thick paste of mashed peas with much salt. The most common drinks were buttermilk and ale, a kind of dark beer.

For rich persons, the day began with a breakfast of white rolls and butter, smoked herring, and whole milk. For lunch, toast with honey, cinnamon biscuits, and warm milk were served. At the main meal, the rich enjoyed boiled cod, barbecued chicken, apple fritters, roast beef or deer meat, bread-coated trout fried in almond oil, and small custard tarts.

Nobles in the medieval period liked hot,

A medieval feast

spicy gravies and rich pudding flavored with honey. Popular dishes included stuffed piglets and multicolored jellies. Red, yellow, green, and purple dyes were made from plants and used to color the jellies, as well as custards.

Some medieval banquets were as grand as the great feasts of ancient Rome. One medieval wedding feast had 406 loaves of bread, 250 eggs, 100 pounds of cheese, 12 quarters of oxen, 16 quarters of mutton, 37 capons, 11 chickens, 2 boar heads and feet. Pigeons and waterfowl, too many to count, were also served.

At some special feasts, roasted peacocks were served, looking as if they were still alive. The peacock's feathers were removed and saved, and the bird was roasted and cooled. When the peacock was arranged on the serving platter, all the saved feathers were put back on the bird to delight the guests.

Swans stuffed with small roasted birds were served wearing gold-coated feathers and crowns of garland. A vinegary hot sauce was served with the swan meat.

During this time, all over Europe, air-dried Norwegian fish, most often cod or haddock, was popular. It was called stockfish, and it was cheap and edible for years after being cured. Before it could be eaten, it had to be beaten with a wooden hammer for a long time to be softened. Once soft, it was soaked in water and boiled for many hours.

A book of table manners was published to remind the noble class to behave themselves at the table. Unacceptable table manners included speaking or singing while your mouth was full of food or drink, leaning your elbows on the table as you ate, picking your teeth with a knife, and blowing on hot food to cool it. Picking up a corner of the tablecloth to wipe your greasy fingers or mouth was also unacceptable, as were gnawing on bones and tearing meat apart with fingers. We follow many of the same table manners today.

Half the world has always lived on wheat, barley, rye, corn, and oats, while the other half lives on rice. Corn has been called the real gold of the Americas. It was first grown thousands of years ago by selective breeding of wild grass. European explorers of the New World were amazed to find vast fields of yellow, red, blue, black, speckled, and flesh-colored corns. Native Americans introduced the Pilgrims to corn on the cob, popcorn, and hominy. Because the natives shared, colonists of the New World were able to survive.

Food choices around the world always depended highly on what was available in an area. Because we now have the ability to ship all kinds of food to the far corners of the earth, this is less important, but it is still a major factor. Many people are not wealthy enough to have foods shipped in, so they still rely on what their environment has to offer.

Chapter 4

The Asian Way to Eat

China has been described as a culture more interested in food than any other on Earth. The most common Chinese greeting, "Chi fan le mei you?" translates as "Have you eaten yet?" The Chinese have a unique way of looking at food. Sauces must make the taste of what is being served better, but the food cannot be overpowered by the sauce. Food is seen as something important that can prevent and cure illness. In east Asia, the lack of meat resulted in a type of cuisine that uses small bits of vegetables, fish, and poultry in a very imaginative and delicious way.

The first restaurant opened in China about 5,000 years ago. Chinese travelers stopped off to rest at Buddhist monasteries, and out of this custom came the roadside inn. About 1,000 years ago, the European adventurer

Marco Polo told of China's many taverns and teahouses.

Great banquets featuring many kinds of food were served in China, as they were in other cultures. In wealthy homes, meals might include as many as forty courses. The first dishes were brought to the dining room to show off the skill of the chef. They were beautifully-arranged dishes of food meant for decoration, and they were not eaten. A Chinese cookbook from 1,500 years ago explained that the kitchen must always be located at the back of the house. That way, the smoke from the kitchen and the noise of clanging pots and pans would not disturb the people in the front of the house.

Dim sum is a popular kind of dining in China. The words mean "touch the heart." Dim sum is a variety of small, delicious snacks such as pork, seafood, and vegetables for guests to sample. One can have a full meal by tasting a little bit of everything.

Chinese food is eaten with chopsticks. The Chinese word for this translates as "quick brothers". Chopsticks have been made of silver, gold, ivory, wood, and bamboo. Today they are often made of plastic. Chopsticks are used for both cooking and eating. Chinese chopsticks have blunt ends.

Rice is a plentiful grain that is served at every meal. For breakfast, people eat a thin rice dish with peanuts, scrambled eggs, and bean cakes. For lunch and the evening meals, there is a bowl of rice with small bits of meat, fish, and vegetables.

Sweets are not served with meals in China, but between meals, the Chinese enjoy sweet snacks, which include small cakes, pastries, fruits, and steamed sweet potatoes. These are often bought from the many street vendors. The national beverage is hot, unsweetened tea, normally drunk from a small cup.

In China, and other parts of Asia, rice is always eaten, but street vendors will offer tempting silkworm grubs that are steamed and piping hot. Some people enjoy cooked scorpions. Barbecued snake is also a tasty treat. Fish paste is common throughout

A street vendor offers cooked scorpions.

southeast Asia. It is made by gathering shrimp or anchovies in a mound, mixing them with salt, and leaving the mixture in the sun for a while. Paste is made when the liquid is pressed out.

In Thailand, a popular item is jackfruit. This bright-yellow, oval-shaped fruit has a spongy, velvety texture and a very strong odor. It can be up to 3 feet long and 20 inches

33

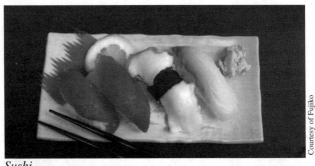
Sushi

wide. The rind is green, knobby, and scaled, but the flesh is pink, sweet, and fragrant.

The Japanese call their cooking sappari (sa-PA-ree), which means "clean, light, neat, and sparkling." Cooking and serving food is considered a fine art. Food must be attractive to the eye as well as good to eat. In Japan, as in China, food is eaten with chopsticks, but Japanese chopsticks have pointed ends.

Seafood is extremely popular in Japan. Sashimi (sa-SHEE-mee) is thinly-sliced fish, eaten raw. As in lobster restaurants in the United States, the diners get to see the fish swimming around in a tank; they can choose their dinner while it is still alive. One well-known dish, Sushi (SOO-shee), are small cakes of cold rice seasoned with vinegar

34

and topped with slices of raw fish, usually served with wasabi (wah-SAH-bee), a spicy-hot green horseradish paste.

Maybe the most dangerous food in Japan is fugu (FOO-goo), or blowfish. Although it is a delicacy, its organs are poisonous and must be removed before the fish is eaten. Chefs who serve fugu must have a license from the government. The poison in the fish's organs is so deadly that if any of it gets into the food to be served, it can be fatal. A number of persons die every year in Japan from the improper handling of blowfish.

Unusual food found in the Philippines includes diniguan (din-ih-GWAN), or blood stew. It is made from the meat or insides of a pig as well as pig blood. To make it sound better, it is sometimes called chocolate pork. Another Filipino dish is kare-kare (KAR-ay KAR-ay), a meaty oxtail stew. This soup mixes vegetables and pieces of tender tripe (stomach lining) in peanut sauce.

Chapter 5

African, Near Eastern, Indian, and Australian Tastes

Those who live in northern and central Africa eat couscous (KOOS-koos), which is made from hard wheat flour. It is made into a spicy mixture by the addition of strong seasonings. Sometimes, nuts and fruits are added to make it sweeter.

Throughout Africa, meat is eaten. The type depends on the livestock available. In some dry, treeless areas, insects are a very important part of the diet, as they have been in almost every part of the world at some time. Many people who eat locusts and grubs would be horrified to learn that others eat raw oysters or the flesh of pigs.

Fufu, a popular food in western Africa, is made from pounded yams that are served with peanut sauce. Much African food is spicy hot. The popular African seasoning

Shish-kebab

called pilli-pilli (PIL-ee PIL-ee) is stronger than cayenne (ky-EN) pepper and is believed not only to make foods delicious but to help prevent illness.

Foods of Near Eastern peoples, like the Arabs, Persians, Turks, Syrians, and Greeks, usually include shish-kebab (SHISH-keh-bob), which consists of alternating pieces of meat and vegetables broiled on skewers. Many of us serve shish-kebab today at our own backyard barbecues. Grape leaves stuffed with meat and rice are common in Near Eastern countries. A delicious treat is baklava (bah-kleh-VAH), a flaky pastry rolled with nuts and drizzled with honey

Whitchety grub is an Australian treat. It is the larva of a kind of moth.

and syrup.

In India, the people continue to cook as they did in ancient times. Foods are richly seasoned with spices to make curry. Yogurt and rice appear at every meal. For the poor, rice may be the only food, but even among the wealthy, huge dinners with a variety of foods are not very common.

In Australia, kangaroo meat is eaten. It has been described as a sweet, strong-tasting meat with a texture somewhere between that of deer meat and liver. One unusual Australian treat is witchety grubs, a plump insect served in many restaurants.

Chapter 6

New Foods of the New World

Peppers from top to bottom: Long Green Pepper, Jalepeno, Sorrento

Christopher Columbus found foods like allspice, maize (corn) and also lima beans in the New World. People who came after him would be introduced to avocados, pineapples, and tomatoes.

The Caribbean islands where Columbus landed had some of the hottest sauces in the world. They were made from chili peppers. Cassava is grown everywhere. This large vegetable looks like a cylinder and has white flesh under the thick and barklike skin. From the blend of Arawak (AR-eh-wak) and Caribbean cultures came a variety of food. The Arawak people began what is now a

39

very popular kind of food preparation— jerk cooking. Meat is seasoned and then smoked, until it is dry. The final product is called "Jerky," which comes from a Native American word. Because it does not spoil quickly, it was very important in the days before refrigerators.

In South America, there originated a great variety of food, like corn, potatoes, beans, strawberries, peanuts, pineapples, as well as tomatoes. The mighty Inca Empire, which stretched from modern-day Ecuador to the middle of Chile on the Pacific Coast, grew many of these foods. Among these foods, potatoes were especially important and would become the main food for much of Europe in later centuries. Other regions of the South American continent, such as the Amazon jungle, had less agriculture. The people there had to rely on hunting and gathering. In some cases, this was because natural food was so plentiful, but it is also very difficult to farm in tropical jungles.

Despite the variety of food, the main

Corn and Potatoes

crops of Central and South America were potatoes and corn. Both of these grow quickly and easily, but both foods have problems. Potatoes do not last long in storage, and plant diseases can often easily destroy them. When these diseases arise, humans can starve. In the 1800s, the potato crop of Ireland was destroyed by a disease, and many people died in areas where the potato was the main source of food. Corn is not very nutritious in comparison to other crops, and people who eat only corn suffer from severe nutritional problems.

Aztec feasts were as splendid as any in the ancient world. At royal banquets, the Aztec ruler was given hundreds of dishes, which he ate behind a silk screen. Women prepared the food, however only men were welcomed at the banquets. Every meal at the palace ended with a chocolate drink that

41

had a foamy head, which was made when the liquid was poured from a great height. Aztec seasonings included blue verbena flowers, to sweeten the food, and magnolia flowers, which taste like ripe melons. The chocolate drinks were flavored with these seasonings. Both the Mayas and the Aztecs thought frog legs and tadpoles fried in cornmeal were great delicacies. The Aztecs bred a certain type of dog for food and served it only with vegetables, as a special treat at royal banquets.

In Mexico, the tortilla (tor-TEE-uh) is very important. Tortillas are little cakes made from rubbing corn kernels into a paste that is then slapped into a thin, round pancake and cooked. At mealtimes, the sounds of women slapping the tortillas into shape can be heard everywhere. Tortillas are wrapped around meat, chicken, fish, and sometimes beans and vegetables. With mild or hot sauces added, they are eaten like a sandwich.

Seviche (seh-VEE-chay), raw fish that is marinated in citrus juice overnight, is the

The prickly pear is commonly eaten in Mexico.

traditional recipe of many Mexican coastal towns. Also popular in Mexico is tequila, a liquor that is made from a cactus called agave. Tequila worms are sold in tiny bottles. The worm, called the gusano (goo-SA-no), lives on the agave plants from which tequila is made. Some people say it is very tasty. The extremely hot jalapeño (hal-leh-PAY-nyo) pepper is popular in Mexico. Its heat can come as a real shock to someone who is not ready for it and can send him or her running towards the water faucet. The bright green habanero (hah-beh-NARE-oh) pepper is even hotter.

Prickly pear cactus salad is common throughout Mexico and the southwestern United States. The flat, oval-shaped, prickly green pads of the cactus are sometimes called beaver tails, which are what they look like.

Chapter 7

Foods of the Native Americans

Native Americans in Alaska ate local fish and animals. Ducks, seagulls, caribou, seals, and walrus were all used. Even polar bears were eaten. The Eskimos made a dish called "stinkheads." They cut the heads off sea salmon and buried them in the ground for the summer. In the winter, they dug them up and ate them, even though they had a very strong odor.

The Eskimos of Alaska made ice cream by grating reindeer tallow (TA-loe), which is fat. While slowly adding seal oil to the fat, they beat it. Finally, the mix got white and fluffy. Berries were added to give it taste and sweetness. Because the winters were long and cold, reindeer-tallow ice cream kept very well.

Tribes in the coastal northwest used kelp, seaweed that they called tangleweed, to wrap

Pemmican is a mixture of dried meat, fat, and fruit.

all kinds of foods, which were then broiled. The kelp gave the food a unique flavor.

Among Native Americans in the southeastern United States, alligator was viewed as a delicacy. It was fried with peppers and onions. Alligator meat is fine and white and has almost no fat. It has been described as a cross between catfish, chicken, and frogs' legs, with a mild, distinctive flavor of its own.

Native peoples of the high plains made pemmican (PEH-mih-kehn), an excellent long-lasting food they could take with them wherever they went. Lean, jerked, dried meat, often buffalo, was pounded and was mixed with fat, wild fruit, and seeds to make a thick paste that was shaped into cakes or balls. The pemmican was carried in buckskin bags and eaten as it was, or sometimes added to a stew.

Because it is so useful—as an emergency food, for example—pemmican is still made today. Companies make it as a product for sale, and people make it in their own homes.

Chapter 8

Pilgrims and Pioneers Learn How to Eat

One of history's most famous voyages took place because people disliked eating bland food; they wanted to "spice it up." The "Indies," near India, had many spices, and Europeans wanted to find a way to get to the Indies as quickly as possible, to bring those spices back home. At the time, a pound of ginger was as valuable as a whole sheep. A pound of cloves was the equal of seven sheep or cows. A sack of pepper was so valuable it was almost priceless.

A young Italian sailor called Christopher Columbus told Queen Isabella of Spain he could find a shorter route to the Indies. He needed the queen to pay for his journey, and she agreed. Columbus did not find the shorter route, but he found something far more important—the spice-rich islands of the Caribbean, which came to be called the

47

"West Indies." (The old Indies, near India, were renamed "the East Indies.")

Of course, the islands of the Caribbean were just a small part of Columbus's "New World." Colonists from England moved to that world, and part of it eventually became the United States.

The Native peoples of America taught the colonists to make cornmeal. They also taught them which vegetables to plant. Beans, squash, and potatoes became the main part of the pioneer diet. Although the Native Americans cooked over an open fire, indoor kitchens quickly became a part of the pioneer cabin. The black cookstove, which was always kept burning, used wood or whatever else was available for fuel. In the treeless West, dried droppings of buffalo, oxen, and cows were used to keep the fire going. These "chips" were accompanied in the fire by twisted, dried balls of prairie grass.

Pioneer food included cornbread cakes fried in hot fat. These cakes were called corn dodgers or hush puppies. Hogs were cured in salt barrels for several weeks, then the meat was rubbed with pepper and molasses and smoked over a fire. Cured hams could be kept for a year without spoiling.

The thrifty pioneers wasted nothing. They made headcheese, which is boiled and pressed meat from the pig's head, liver, heart, and tongue. Pig bladders were used to cover jars of canned fruit and vegetables—or sometimes were blown up like balloons for children to play with. The youngest child in the pioneer family got to eat the pig's tail, which was cooked over an open fire. Even the pigs' feet were pickled in vinegar.

In the early days of the American West, the Lewis and Clark expedition journeyed from St. Louis, Missouri, to Oregon. The team set off on the long trip well supplied with two tons of sugar, corn, beans, lard, flour, and cured pork. On the journey, unleavened bread and a saltless hard biscuit called hardtack were baked over an open fire. Team members hunted and fished. One

One buffalo provided four hundred pounds of meat.

adult bison, or as Lewis and Clark called it, buffalo, provided four hundred pounds of meat for the men, who often ate nine pounds of meat in a day.

Cooking a buffalo that had been killed by one of the men in the expedition was a huge chore. First, a fire was built in a pit; then stones were laid on top of the fire. The stones were covered with pine branches, on which the buffalo meat was laid. The meat was covered with more pine branches, and water was poured over everything, but not enough to put out the fire in the pit. On top of this, four inches of soil was put, and the buffalo meat cooked in this strange oven.

For three hours, the meat roasted, and it came out tender and juicy. Unfortunately, explorer Meriwether Lewis complained, it did not taste anything like buffalo; it tasted like a pine tree.

In California, during the gold rush of 1849, miners found that the water in the area was muddy and filled with germs. It tasted awful. Miners added molasses, white wine, vinegar, and ground ginger to it, to improve its taste. This mixture was called switchel

When some enterprising Chinese people opened restaurants in the gold fields, the miners crowded in and ate beef and deer meat, along with special treats from China. Those included stewed seaweed, shark fins, scorpion eggs, and bamboo shoots.

Countries like Australia, Argentina, Canada, and the United States had and still do have huge rangelands that make it possible for people to eat a lot of beef.

Chapter 9

Foods of Europe

Food in Europe is as different as the many different regions in which it is grown, harvested, and eaten. Each country offers its own unique specialties.

In Greece, a white wine called retsina actually has pine resin or sap added to it. In Tuscany, Italy, cockscombs are served. In many parts of Italy, songbirds are roasted and served whole. Italian food relies heavily on pasta, which is dried dough in the form of spaghetti, noodles, macaroni, and ravioli. Small restaurants called pizzerias (PEET-seh-ree-ehz) feature circles of dough that are covered with tomato sauce, cheese, herbs, and other toppings and then baked in hot ovens. The Italian pizza has made its way to many other parts of the world and has become one of the most popular party foods in the United States.

Fermented shark meat hangs to dry in an Iceland shed.

In Iceland, a special food is hakarl (how-carrhl), the fermented meat of a local shark. The shark is poisonous when fresh, so the meat is carefully handled. In the old days it was buried deep in the ground for the fermentation period. In modern times, it is packed in air-tight plastic and left to ferment for several weeks. Once fermented, the meat is hung out to dry. Finally, it is cut into bite-sized cubes and eaten with toothpicks.

Food from Germany is rich and hearty. Sauerbraten (ZAU-er-brah-ten), a sweet-and-sour pot roast that is often served with sauerkraut (ZAU-er-krowt), a type of sour cabbage with a very distinctive smell.

53

The word delicatessen (deh-lih-keh-TEH-sehn) comes from a German word meaning "delicate eating."

German cooks also gave the world hamburgers. Americans were introduced to hamburgers when German immigrants first arrived in Cincinnati, Ohio. A hamburger on a bun first got a lot of attention at the St. Louis Exposition in 1904. Hamburgers have been tremendously successful. Billions are sold every year in the United States.

In Great Britain, breakfast is a big meal. Often there is fish, hot cereal, and broiled ham or bacon. Tea is the most popular drink. Afternoon tea is served with cakes, pastries, and hot breads or crumpets. Crumpets are small, round, unsweetened breads cooked on a griddle and then toasted. This "tea time" relieves hunger in the midafternoon, before the evening meal. A popular British snack is "bubble and squeak," a strange name for fried vegetables.

France is well-known for raising the art of cooking to high levels. Food in the fine

French style is called "haute cuisine" (oat kwee-ZEEN), which means high cooking, and French restaurants are famous for their marvelous dishes. A good French cook can turn ordinary products like meat, fish, and vegetables into masterpieces by the skillful use of herbs and seasonings and the proper use of cooking wine. The long, thin crusty loaves of bread carried home daily by the French are an essential part of every meal. This kind of bread is called a baguette. They are often eaten with French cheeses. People shop daily for meats, vegetables, and, of course, bread, which shows that freshness is very important for the French.

Special French dishes are often named for persons or places. An example is "chicken Morengo," which was created in 1800, when the French general Napoleon Bonaparte had just defeated the Austrians in the Battle of Marengo in Italy. Napoleon was hungry, but the army's supply train had not yet caught up with the troops. Some soldiers were sent to find food for Napoleon. All they could come up with were one small chicken, three eggs, four tomatoes, and six crayfish. The items were cooked in garlic and oil and served to him with bread and brandy. Napoleon was so delighted by the dish that from then on it was frequently served to him. It is now a popular dish all over the world.

Chapter 10

Food in the United States

Because Americans come from so many different cultures, people in the United States can buy almost any kind of food they want. Enormous supermarkets offer a huge selection of foods. There are also a lot of ethnic markets in large cities. These little markets specialize in preparing and selling foods from certain areas or countries.

Special dishes are found in every state and in many different regions of the United States. Most of them came with immigrants who settled in the particular areas. One example of this is the many Polish people who settled on the eastern end of Long Island. Polish foods like kielbasa (kill-BAH-suh), which is a spicy smoked sausage, and pierogies (per-O-gees), which is dough stuffed with potatoes, cheese, or other fillings, are very popular there. Because many Germans and

Swedish immigrants moved to Wisconsin and Minnesota, many markets sell a variety of sausages, cheeses, and Scandinavian fish.

In the South, there are foods not usually found in other parts of the United States. Crawfish, grits, chitterlings, and fried pork bits are quite popular. Hog snouts and chicken feet were eaten, pickled whole and in soup. Chicken-fried steak, which is beef covered with flour batter and fried like chicken, is a southern favorite.

Soul food, which is popular among black Americans, originated in the slave kitchens of the South. Some favorites are smothered cabbage, the feet, snouts, and ears of pigs, and turnip greens along with ham hocks and bacon drippings. Soul food is like most other southern cooking since it is highly seasoned, heavily cooked, and very tasty.

In the western United States, fried pork rinds, blood-rare steaks, and rattlesnake meat are popular. Recipes for preparing rattlesnake advise the cook to cut the flesh in chunks and roll the chunks in a batter of flour, cracker meal, salt, pepper, and garlic. The pieces are deep fried until they turn golden brown.

In the Midwest, fruitcakes remain very popular. Many people all over the country enjoy this heavy cake, which is filled with nuts and brightly-colored candied fruits. Others insist that the only use for a fruitcake is as a doorstop!

In the eastern United States, pork loaf is common, and so is seafood, along the coast. The mid-Atlantic region is well known for its crabcakes. In the Northeast, fried scrapple served with eggs and plenty of maple syrup is a favorite dish. Scrapple is meat scraps cooked in corn meal, and some people fear it contains animal parts one would not want to eat. Also common in the Northeast are lobsters, raw oysters, creamy clam chowder, and fiddlehead ferns.

In Hawaii, some of the local people still prepare their own special dishes. Some of the unusual foods in Hawaii include pickled lily bulbs and dried seaweed served with duck. Poi (poy) is a well-known Hawaiian specialty. It is a paste made from the taro root. Poi has a slightly sour taste, and some critics have compared it with glue. It has a light lavender color, and is very popular when sweetened with sugar.

At a luau (LOO-ow) in Hawaii, the main course is often a suckling pig, cooked on stones in a deep pit. The pig is cooked whole, usually with an apple in its mouth. It is served with many of Hawaii's delicious fruits, like pineapples, breadfruit, coconuts, and bananas.

All over the United States there are food products that strangers might find quite remarkable. Red, green, and purple breakfast cereals have become widespread. Candies that look like worms, spiders, and centipedes are quite popular, especially with children. Chewing gum, once made from chicle, the sap of a Central American tree, is now usually made with plastics to which artificial sweeteners and colors have been added. In the search for tasty and attractive

Fast food is an example of fatty American food.

foods, products are often highly processed and include man-made ingredients with ever more sugar, salt, and fat.

People are becoming more and more concerned with their health these days, and the way we eat is changing. We now look for fresh fruits and vegetables that have not been sprayed with bug killers. We want meat that has little or no fat. Our breads and cereals need to contain more whole grains and fiber. We look for foods that are higher in protein and lower in fat. We pay more attention to the food pyramid and try to eat more servings of healthful foods, while we cut down on fat and sweets. In some ways,

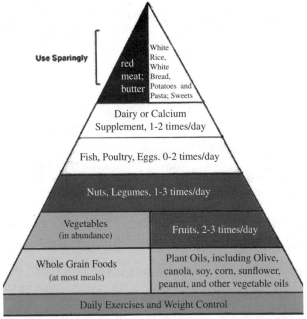

Food pyramids give advice on what is healthy to eat.

we have gone back to eating the way cave dwellers did thousands of years ago. The foods ancient people ate because they didn't have anything else—wholesome, pure, and natural foods—are becoming our foods of choice.

Bibliography

Cox, Beverly, and Martin Jacobs. Spirit of the Harvest: North American Indian Cooking. New York: Stewart, Tabori & Chang, 2001.

Dawson, Imogen. Food and Feasts in Ancient Greece. Parsippany, N.J.: New Discovery Books, 1995.

Dosier, Susan. Colonial Cooking. Mankato, Minn.: Blue Earth Books, 2000.

Gunderson, Mary. Cooking on the Lewis and Clark Expedition: Exploring History Through Simple Recipes. Mankato, Minn.: Blue Earth Books, 2000.

Gunderson, Mary. The Food Journal of Lewis and Clark. Yankton, South Dakota: History Cooks, 2002.

Gunderson, Mary. Pioneer Farm Cooking. Mankato, Minn.: Blue Earth Books, 2000.

James, Simon. Ancient Rome. New York: Viking, 1992.

Kavasch, E. Barrie. Enduring Harvest. Old Saybrook, Conn,: Globe Pequot Press, 1995.

Lukins, Sheila. All Around the World Cookbook. New York: Workman Publishing, 1994.

Pearson, Anne. The Vikings. New York: Viking Press, 1994.

Smith, Jeff. The Frugal Gourmet Cooks Three Ancient Cuisines: China, Greece, and Rome. New York: W. Morrow, 1989.

Vezza, Diane Simone. Passport on a Plate: A Round-the-World Cookbook for Children. New York: Simon and Schuster, 1997.

Von Hagen, Victor W. Realm of the Incas. New York: New American Library, 1957.